Bass Cla Student

MW01222263

by Neal Porter in collaboration with Fred Weber

To The Student

This book, with the aid of a good teacher, is designed to help you become an excellent player on your instrument in a most enjoyable manner. It will take a reasonable amount of work and CAREFUL practice on your part. If you do this, learning to play should be a valuable and pleasant experience.

To The Teacher

The Belwin "Student Instrumental Course" is the first and only complete course for individual instruction of all band instruments. Like instruments may be taught in classes. Cornets, trombones, baritones, and basses may be taught together. The course is designed to give the student a sound musical background and at the same time provide for the highest degree of interest and motivation. The entire course is correlated to the band oriented sequence.

To make the course both authoritative and practical, most books are co-authored by a national authority of each instrument in collaboration with Fred Weber, perhaps the most widely-known and accepted authority at the student level.

The Belwin "Student Instrumental Course" has three levels: elementary, intermediate, and advanced intermediate. Each level consists of a method and three correlating supplementary books. In addition, a duet book is available for Flute, Bb Clarinet, Eb Alto Sax, Bb Cornet and Trombone. The chart below shows the correlating books available with each part.

The Belwin "STUDENT INSTRUMENTAL COURSE" — A course for individual and class instruction of LIKE instruments, at three levels, for all band instruments.

EACH BOOK IS COMPLETE IN ITSELF BUT ALL BOOKS ARE CORRELATED WITH EACH OTHER

METHOD
The Bb Bass Clarinet Student
For individual or Bass Clarinet class instruction.

ALTHOUGH EACH BOOK CAN BE USED SEPARATELY, IDEALLY, ALL SUPPLEMENTARY BOOKS SHOULD BE USED AS COMPANION BOOKS WITH THE METHOD

STUDIES AND MELODIOUS ETUDES

Supplementary scales, warm-up and technical drills, musicianship studies and melody-like studies.

TUNES FOR TECHNIC

Technical type melodies, variations, and "famous passages" from musical literature — for the development of technical dexterity.

THE BASS CLARINET SOLOIST

Interesting and playable graded easy solo arrangements of famous and well-liked melodies. Also contains 2 Duets, and 1 Trio. Easy piano accompaniments.

Elementary Fingering Chart

● — Indicates hole closed, or keys to be pressed.

○ — Indicates hole open.

■ When a number is given, refer to the picture of the Bass Clarinet for additional key to be pressed.

■ When two notes are given together (F and G), they are the same tone and, of course, played the same way.

■ When there are two fingerings given for a note, use the first one unless your teacher tells you otherwise.

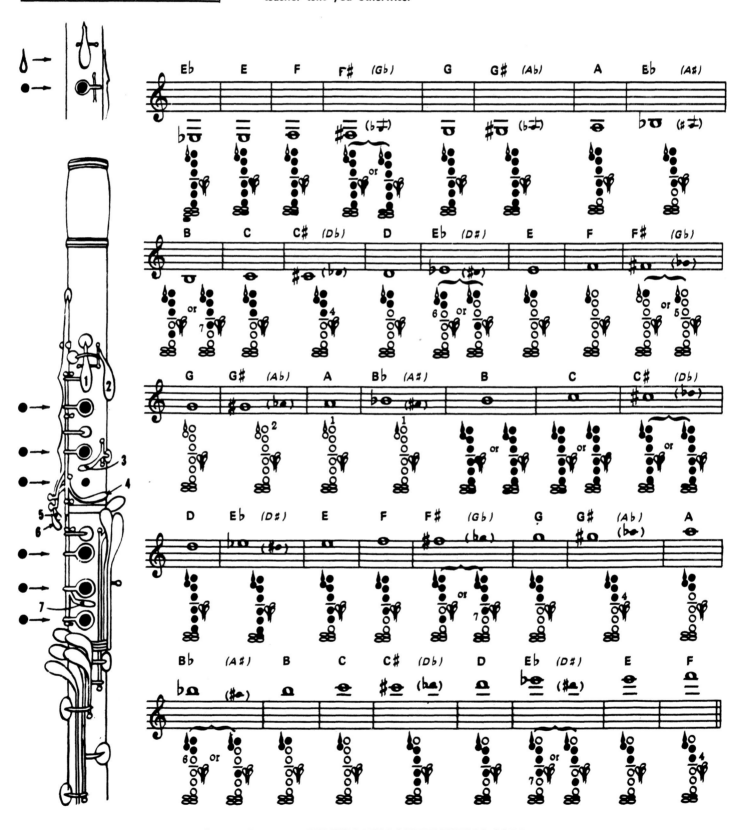

B.I.C. 116

Getting Started

Your teacher will show you how to produce a tone on your bass clarinet.

He will show you the correct position of the Mouth, Hands, and Fingers.

It Is Very Important that you hold the instrument properly.

WHEN YOU HAVE THE CORRECT PLAYING POSITION, FOLLOW THESE STEPS:

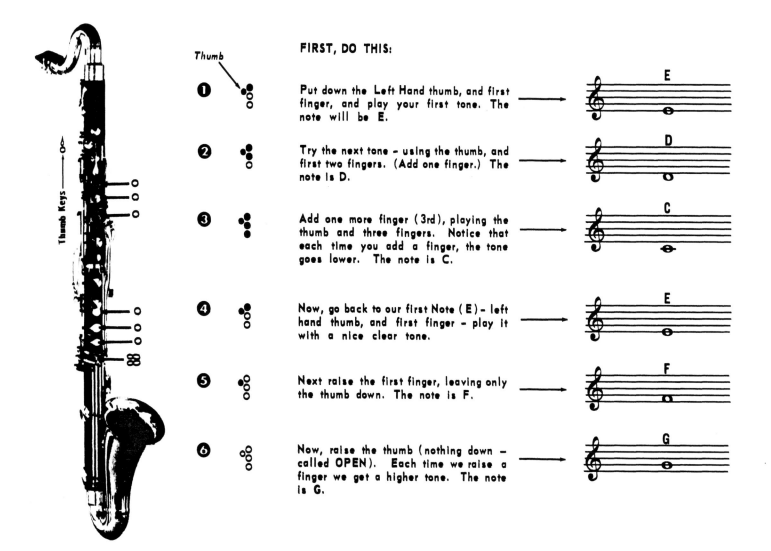

FIRST, DO THIS:

❶ Put down the Left Hand thumb, and first finger, and play your first tone. The note will be E. → **E**

❷ Try the next tone - using the thumb, and first two fingers. (Add one finger.) The note is D. → **D**

❸ Add one more finger (3rd), playing the thumb and three fingers. Notice that each time you add a finger, the tone goes lower. The note is C. → **C**

❹ Now, go back to our first Note (E) - left hand thumb, and first finger - play it with a nice clear tone. → **E**

❺ Next raise the first finger, leaving only the thumb down. The note is F. → **F**

❻ Now, raise the thumb (nothing down - called OPEN). Each time we raise a finger we get a higher tone. The note is G. → **G**

NEXT, DO THIS:

Practice the notes below until you can play them with ease. Play each note with a nice clear sound.

GOING UP   **GOING DOWN**

Lesson 1   Reading Music

You should know the following rudiments before starting to play:

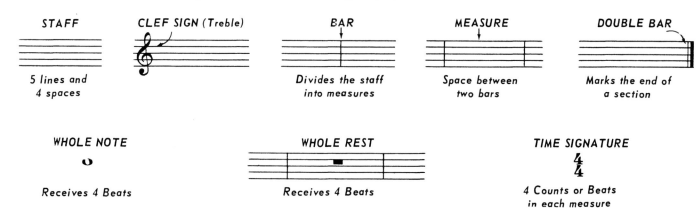

STAFF	CLEF SIGN (Treble)	BAR	MEASURE	DOUBLE BAR
5 lines and 4 spaces		Divides the staff into measures	Space between two bars	Marks the end of a section

WHOLE NOTE	WHOLE REST	TIME SIGNATURE
Receives 4 Beats	Receives 4 Beats	$\frac{4}{4}$ 4 Counts or Beats in each measure

→ Notes and Musical Terms used for the first time are pointed out with ARROWS.
They should be memorized.

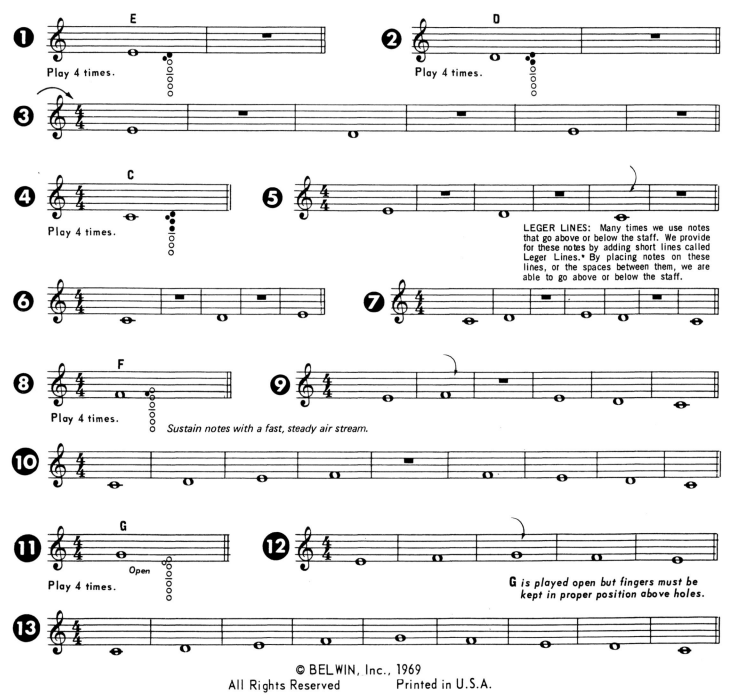

LEGER LINES: Many times we use notes that go above or below the staff. We provide for these notes by adding short lines called Leger Lines.* By placing notes on these lines, or the spaces between them, we are able to go above or below the staff.

Sustain notes with a fast, steady air stream.

G is played open but fingers must be kept in proper position above holes.

© BELWIN, Inc., 1969
All Rights Reserved   Printed in U.S.A.

Lesson 2

QUARTER NOTE 1 count.

BREATH MARK - means to breathe.

❶ 1 2 3 4   1 2 3 4

For the first few pages, name and finger the notes before you play each line.

QUARTER REST 1 count.

❷

❸

Correct tonguing (articulation) is very important. Discuss it with your teacher. Most teachers prefer to have the top of the tip of your tongue contact lightly under the very tip of the reed. There are various ways of satisfactory tonguing. See which one your teacher prefers.

❹

❺ ❻

Do not breath during every rest. Breath only when needed.

❼

Keep cheeks in at all times. Do not let them puff out.

Merrily We Roll Along

❽

Fingers must be relaxed and curved at all times.

❾

Practice playing down the scale below C the right hand, one after the other, so you with the lower tones and your fingers will position. All holes above the last open hole, must be as you go down.

with the fingers of will become familiar adjust to the correct completely closed

Start with C then first finger of the right hand, then 2nd, 3rd and 4th.

The 4th finger goes on the key indicated in this diagram.

See photo No. 2, Page 3 and Chart, Page 2.

If you have trouble getting some of the tones it is probably because your embouchure is too tight or your mouthpiece is not far enough in your mouth. Discuss this with your teacher. Practice running down and up until you can do it with ease and with a nice clear tone. We will learn the names of the notes later.

Put the NUMBER of the LINE or SPACE the note is on, in the square and write below whether the note is on a line or space.

| 1 | | | | | | | | | |

Space _____ _____ _____ _____ _____ _____ _____ _____ _____

Lesson 3

When playing "A" it is best to use the side of the index (first) finger at the first knuckle.

Famous Melody

HALF NOTE 2 counts. **HALF REST** 2 counts.

Half Notes

Count 1 2 3 4 etc.

1 2 3 4 etc.

TIE – 3 Counts (Combines the 2 notes)

Tie

Twinkle Twinkle, Little Star

It is very important for bass clarinet players to always keep the fingers directly above the hole they usually play so when the hole is to be covered, the finger moves only down or up, never sideways. There is never time to feel for a hole before closing it. ALWAYS KEEP THE HANDS AND FINGERS IN PROPER POSITION.

When playing A it is best to use the side of the index finger at about the knuckle so you can roll it slightly to cover the first hole.

PUT THE FOLLOWING ON THE STAFF:

Whole Note	Quarter Note	A Time Signature	Quarter Rest	Half Note	Half Rest	Tie two Notes

Lesson 4

The correct use of the first (index finger) of the left hand when going from E to A or A to E is VERY important. A lot of your success in the future, as a bass clarinet player, will depend upon mastering this position and movement. Discuss this with your teacher.

This may help ... Play bottom line E, using the correct basic position of the left hand, then without moving the position of the hand or fingers, roll the index finger to press the A key and at the same time open the hole for E. The A key is pressed by the side of the index finger at the first knuckle. Roll back again when going from A. to E. Work hard to master this movement correctly. It is very important in developing speed as your playing ability advances.

Lesson 5

You are now ready to begin the companion books, STUDIES AND MELODIOUS ETUDES and TUNES FOR TECHNIC, correlated with the Method as part of the BELWIN STUDENT INSTRUMENTAL COURSE.

Write counting under notes, then play.

London Bridge

Means–Repeat line

¾ Time

TIME – 3 counts in each measure.

4 Counts

Count 1 2 3 1 2 3

Play 1st time only.   Play 2nd time only.

2nd time

The Cuckoo

Review Of Notes

Remember to keep enough mouthpiece in your mouth to get a good clear tone.

❶ Name the notes below.   ❷ Indicate correct fingering.   The 1st one is done for you.

Name   E

Key

Fingering

Lesson 6

As you use your right hand fingers, make certain of a correct right hand thumb position.
The thumb-rest should cradle between the first knuckle and the tip of your thumb.

❶ Low G

Go Tell Aunt Rhode

❷

Twinkle Twinkle Little Star

❸

Lightly Row

❹

Play 2 times. The first time play entire melody - second time, omit notes marked ★ and substitute a quarter rest.

❺

Keep cheeks in at all times.

Drink To Me Only

❻

❼

Counting Fun   **Duet**

(Student)

❽

(Teacher)

❶ Put notes called for on the staff. Use only notes you have learned.   **❷** Indicate fingering.

| F | D | Low B | C | Low A | E | A | G | Low G | Low B | C |

Key

Lesson 7

Slurs

SLUR — Tongue the first note of each slur only. Ask your teacher to explain.

The Mouse Ran Up The Clock

Symphony Melody

DVORAK

1st time only

2nd time only

2nd time

Peter, Peter

PICK-UP NOTE (Ask your teacher to explain.)

A-Tiskit A-Taskit

On the staff below, write the note receiving the number of counts called for (in 4/4 time).

4   2   1   3   1   2   4   2   3   4   2   1   3   4   2   3   1

Lesson 8

Lesson 9

Comparing C And ¢ Time

Jingle Bells

This means the line may be played either in C time or ¢ time. Practice the line in C time until you can play
it well, then play the notes AT THE SAME SPEED but TAP in ¢ time (2 beats per measure).
The notes will sound the same, only the TAPPING will be different.

A Flat (or Sharp) carries through the measure.

KEY SIGNATURE – means all Bs are played B♭. (See note below.)

Notice

Counting Fun

❶ Put in the Bar Lines.   ❷ Write counting under notes.

* Sometimes it is necessary to place a flat at the beginning of a line. This avoids the necessity of placing a flat in front of each B. When there is
a flat in the signature it is always B and the Key is F. The line is in the Key of F because the melody, or study is based on the scale of F.
Until No. 7 on this page there has been no Key Signature. When there is no Key Signature the piece is in the Key of C.

The Jolly Green Giant

Bass Clarinet Solo

B.I.C.116

Lesson 10

You are now ready to play solos from THE BASS CLARINET SOLOIST, a book of solos with Piano Accompaniments correlated with the Method as part of the BELWIN STUDENT INSTRUMENTAL COURSE.

Keep embouchure and air stream steady when changing registers.

Goodnight Ladies

All Bs are played Bb.

Count   3   1   2   3

Fine (Finish)

D.C. al Fine (Go Back to Beginning and Play to Fine.)

Counting Fun

Work out carefully, then try for speed.

Old MacDonald's Duet

Student

Teacher

Both lines played together as a Duet will sound the complete melody. One person can also play both lines for the melody.

Write a **T** below the ties and an **S** below the slurs.

Lesson 11

Lesson 12

You are now ready for DUETS FOR STUDENTS, a book of easy duet arrangements of familiar melodies coordinated with the BELWIN STUDENT INSTRUMENTAL COURSE.

One of the most important things for a young bass clarinetist to master is the correct hand and finger position and movement in going from the low register to the high register, especially between A and B♭ (and similar notes).

Your future ability to play rapidly and smoothly depends to a great extent on mastering this. Correct use of the index finger is vital.

It is equally important to keep the rest of the fingers over the holes and keys at all times so they will be in a position to play B (all fingers down) or other similar tones. The fingers should be in a position so they will only have to move "up" or "down" when playing the holes — never sideways. The right hand fingers SHOULD be left down until you play below G, then they must be lifted.

Your teacher will help you in learning the correct position and the proper hand and finger movements.

Lesson 13

After studying Numbers 9 and 10, can you tell why we use "Key Signatures"?

* When we have 1 sharp in the Key Signature it is always F# and the Key is G. It means the piece is based on the scale of G and all Fs are sharped.

Lesson 14

Eighth Notes

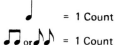

♩ = 1 Count

♫ or ♪♪ = 1 Count

❶

Play Number 1 first in $\frac{4}{4}$ time - then in Cut (¢) Time. Then play Number 2 as written. Compare Number 1 played in ¢ time with Number 2 played in eighth notes.

Your teacher will show you his favorite way of counting eighth notes.

❸

Count 1 + 2 + 1 + 2 +

If the foot-tapping method of counting is used make sure the foot comes UP (Up beat) in EXACTLY the MIDDLE of the BEAT.

❹

1 + 2 + 3 + 4 + 1 + 2 + 3 + 4 +   R.H. Down

Skip To M'Lou

❺

1   2   3   4   1   2 + 3   4

❻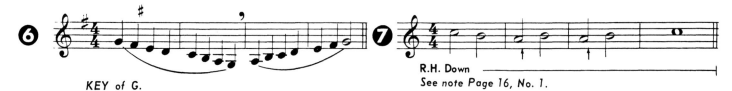

KEY of G.

❼

R.H. Down
See note Page 16, No. 1.

❽

R.H. Down

❾

?   ?

What KEY is this? _____

⓫

R.H. Down

Grandfather's Clock

⓬

This Old Man

⓭

Lesson 15

Old MacDonald

Thirds

Arpeggios

March Theme

What KEY is this?

R.H. Down

Same tempo

Don't Stop.

D#

Lesson 16

Half Step Waltz

SCALE and KEY of G

Bicycle Built For Two

What KEY is this?_____   What KEY?_____   What KEY?_____

Lesson 17

R. Hand Down Throughout.

There's A Hole In The Bucket

What KEY?_____

3 + 1 2 3

What tune is this based on?

Melody In F

RUBINSTEIN

Write the counting under the measures below.

1 2 3 4   1 2 3 4

Lesson 18

is intended to picture a well played tone that doesn't wave and stays on exactly the same pitch.

1

AVOID tones of the type pictured below.

(a) A "Scooped" attack.
(b) A wavy Tone.
(c) Attack not clean.
(d) A Tone that goes flat.
(e) (1) Accented tongue release.
(2) Over-accented attack.

2

Ask your teacher to suggest various ways to slur above line.

3

4

Melody Fun

Play 3 times. The first time play the entire melody. 2nd time - omit all notes marked with ② and substitute a rest.
3rd time - omit all notes marked ② and ③ and substitute quarter rests.

5

To A Wild Rose

MacDOWELL

Soft - slow

Lesson 19

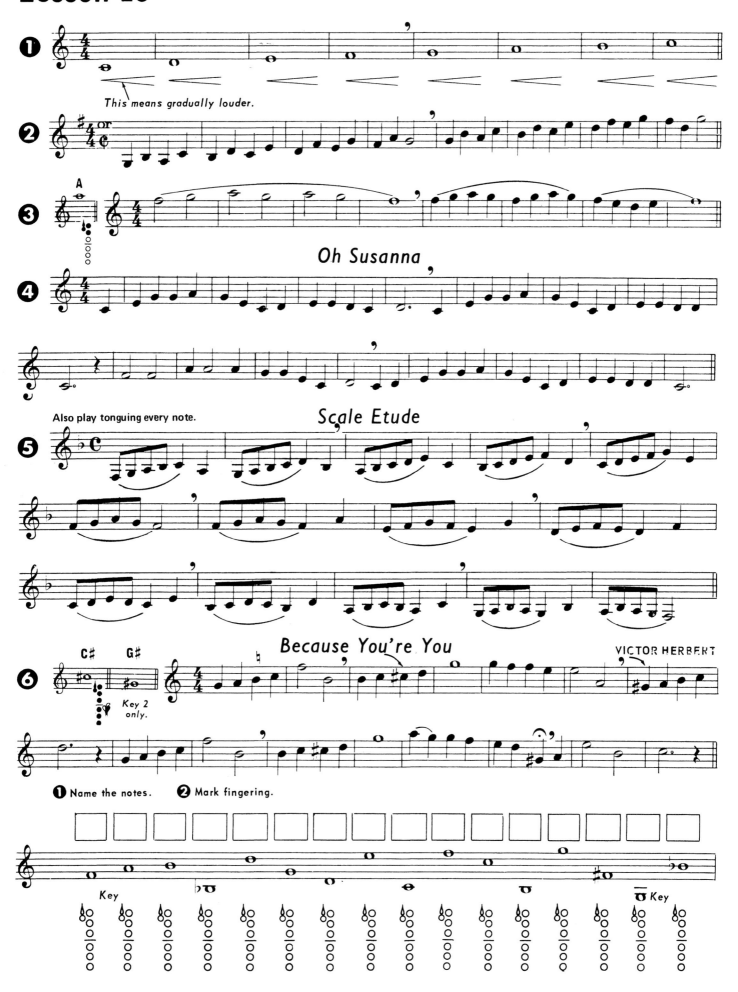

This means gradually louder.

Oh Susanna

Also play tonguing every note.

Scale Etude

Because You're You   VICTOR HERBERT

❶ Name the notes.   ❷ Mark fingering.

Lesson 20

EIGHTH REST - *same time value as eighth note* (♪)   *Staccato - means short or separated.*

Notes with a dot over or under them (♩) are played Staccato. This means to play them short and light. The notes should be separated with a slight rest between each note depending on the character of the piece. *NEVER STOP TONE WITH THE TONGUE.*

Symphony Melody

HAYDN

Work out carefully, then try for speed.   The name of this KEY is? _____

Swing High March

Trio

Lesson 21

Work for a steady tone (as pictured) with no changes of pitch.

Enharmonic Tones

same

Key 2
only.

Work out carefully, then try for speed.   The name of this KEY is? _____

Merry Widow Waltz

LEHAR

R.H. Down

R.H. Down

B.I.C.116

Lesson 22

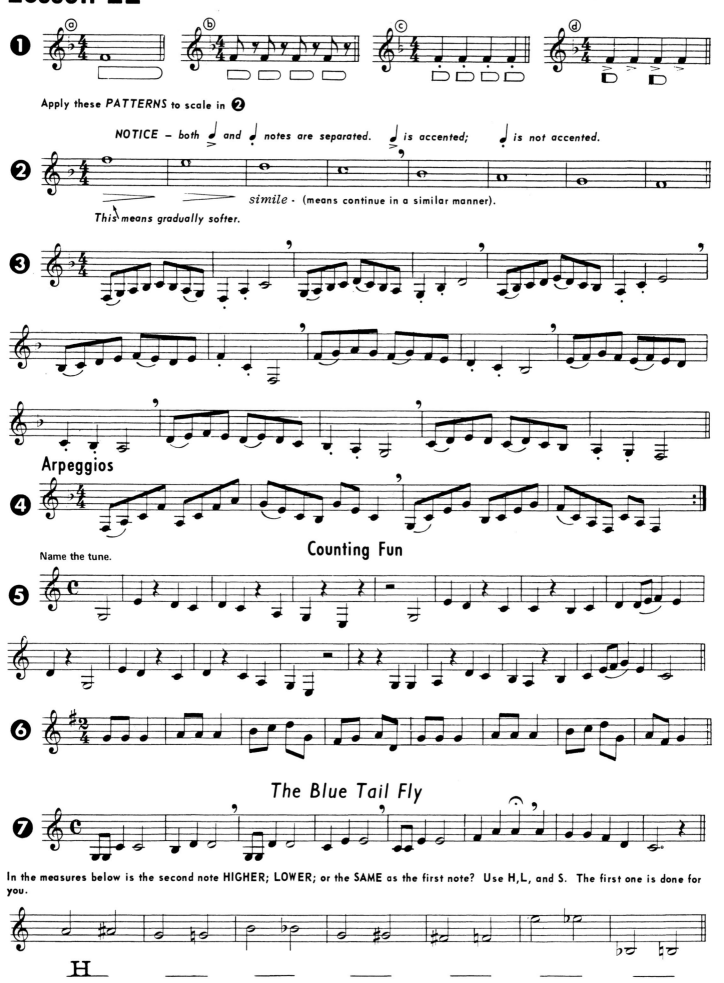

Apply these PATTERNS to scale in ❷

NOTICE – both ♩ and ♩ notes are separated. ♩ is accented; ♩ is not accented.

simile - (means continue in a similar manner).

This means gradually softer.

Arpeggios

Name the tune.

Counting Fun

The Blue Tail Fly

In the measures below is the second note HIGHER; LOWER; or the SAME as the first note? Use H, L, and S. The first one is done for you.

H ___ ___ ___ ___ ___ ___ ___ ___ ___ ___

Lesson 23

1

<svg>< > < > < ></svg> *simile*

Apply each pattern to entire scale in line 1.

① **a**   ② **b**   ③ **c**   *See note below*   ④ **d**

ff mf p

* ♩ stands for *LEGATO* and means to tongue softly with no separation at all between notes.

2   C♯ (D♭)   D♯ (E♭)

------ same ------

same

3

Practice sections individually, then play complete line.

4   **a**   **b**   **c**   **d**

Counting Fun

5

2 + 1 + 2 + 1 + 2 +   etc.

Write counting, then play.

DOTTED QUARTER NOTE

6

1 2 + 3+4 + 1+2 + 3+4 +

The author suggests that you tap twice on the dotted quarter notes (♩.). The eighth note (♪) comes after the 2nd tap, midway between the 2nd and 3rd taps.

America

7

p ← Stands for *PIANO* and means play softly.

Michael, Row The Boat

8

Count   3 4   1 2 + 3   4

mp ← Stands for *MEZZO PIANO* and means to play moderately soft.

Lesson 24

Play staccato 1st time and legato 2nd time.

KEY SIGNATURE – (See note below.)

Notice

KEY of Bb

Auld Lang Syne

What KEY is this?_____

Practice both octaves.

* When there are two flats in the signature, the second flat is always Eb. This means the piece is based on the Bb Scale and all Bs and Es are flatted.

Lesson 25

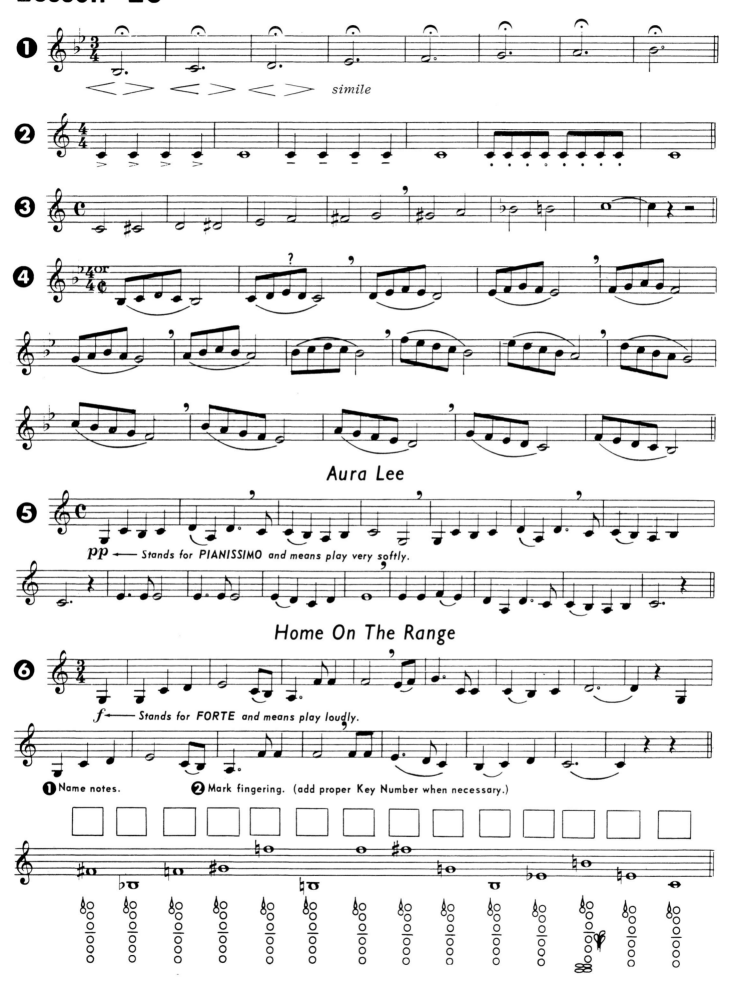

Aura Lee

pp — Stands for PIANISSIMO and means play very softly.

Home On The Range

f — Stands for FORTE and means play loudly.

❶ Name notes.   ❷ Mark fingering. (add proper Key Number when necessary.)

Lesson 26

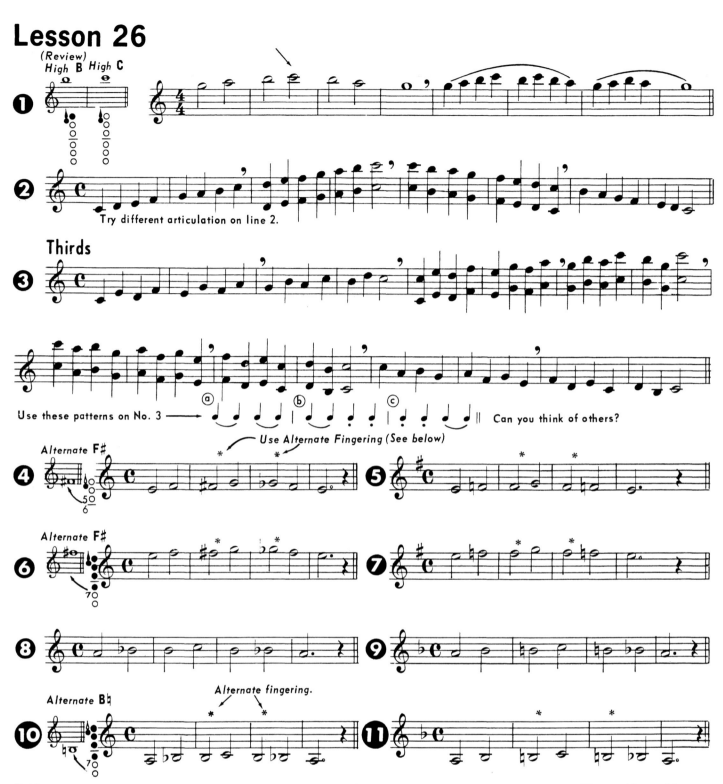

(Review)
High **B** High **C**

Try different articulation on line 2.

Thirds

Use these patterns on No. 3 → (a) (b) (c) ‖ Can you think of others?

Use Alternate Fingering (See below)

Alternate F#

Alternate F#

Alternate B♮

Alternate fingering.

*—This means to use the alternate fingering. Some notes on the clarinet can be fingered more than one way. These additional fingerings are usually called "Alternate Fingerings". This mark * above a note means to use the alternate fingering. It is very important to learn HOW and WHEN to use these alternate fingerings because it leads to faster and smoother playing as you progress. They are absolutely essential in more advanced clarinet playing. See Page 40 for more information on the most important of these alternate fingerings and when to use them.

A Technical Challenge
Clarinet Polka

Alternate F# Work out carefully, then try for speed.

Lesson 27

The Man On The Flying Trapeze

Practice both octaves.

Sweet Betsy From Pike

Lesson 28

Practice both octaves.

$\frac{6}{8}$ Time

$\frac{6}{8}$ TIME is played exactly like $\frac{3}{8}$ Time except there are 6 Counts in each measure.

Count   1 2 3 4 5 6   1 2 3 4 5 6

(♩. = 6 Counts)

Review Etude

Over The Waves

Fun With Counting

Same tempo. ♪ = 1 count

mf ← Stands for MEZZO FORTE and means to play moderately loud.

Don't stop.

Same tempo.

Same tempo.

Lesson 29

My Wild Irish Rose

ALWAYS check Key Signature and Time Signature before playing a line or piece.

Yankee Doodle Boy

ff → Stands for *FORTISSIMO* and means play with a very big tone.

Lesson 30

Lesson 31

William Tell Theme

Moment Musical

American Patrol

Lesson 32

Lesson 33

Apply these rhythms to Scale.

Key 2 only.

Key 2 only.

Trepak

TSCHAIKOWSKY

Variation On A Familiar Theme

---

* When we have three flats in the Key Signature, they are always Bb, Eb, and Ab. The Key is Eb. This means the piece is based on the Scale of Eb and all Bs, Es, and As are flatted.

Basic Technic
Practice as assigned by your Teacher

Basic Technic
Practice as assigned by your teacher.

The Patterns below provide for unlimited scale practice in the 7 most common band keys.
FOLLOW THESE INSTRUCTIONS.

Start with ANY line and play through the entire pattern without stopping. Return to the STARTING LINE and play to where the END is marked. You must keep the KEY SIGNATURE of the STARTING LINE THROUGHOUT the entire pattern.

Chromatic Scales

Also play tongued.

Use Alternate F#

See Chart (Page 2) for fingerings you don't know.

Use Alternate B♮

Alternate Fingerings Used In This Book

Home Practice Record

Week	Mon.	Tues.	Wed.	Thurs.	Fri.	Sat.	Total	Parent's Signature	Week	Mon.	Tues.	Wed.	Thurs.	Fri.	Sat.	Total	Parent's Signature
1									21								
2									22								
3									23								
4									24								
5									25								
6									26								
7									27								
8									28								
9									29								
10									30								
11									31								
12									32								
13									33								
14									34								
15									35								
16									36								
17									37								
18									38								
19									39								
20									40								

B.I.C.116